DOONESBURY.COM'S
The WAR in QUOTES

Introduction by G. B. Trudeau

Edited by David Stanford,
Duty Officer, *Doonesbury* Town Hall

D0104828

Andrews McMeel
Publishing, LLC

Kansas City

DOONESBURY is distributed internationally by Universal Press Syndicate.

The War in Quotes copyright © 2008 by G. B. Trudeau. All rights reserved. Printed in the United States of America. No part of this book may be used or reproduced in any manner whatsoever without written permission except in the case of reprints in the context of reviews. For information, write Andrews McMeel Publishing, LLC, an Andrews McMeel Universal company, 1130 Walnut Street, Kansas City, Missouri 64106.

08 09 10 11 12 MLT 10 9 8 7 6 5 4 3 2 1

ISBN-13: 978-0-7407-7231-3
ISBN-10: 0-7407-7231-7

Library of Congress Control Number: 2008024621

www.andrewsmcmeel.com

DOONESBURY may be viewed on the Internet at
www.doonesbury.com and www.GoComics.com.

Book text design: George Corsillo/Design Monsters

Attention: Schools and Businesses
Andrews McMeel books are available at quantity discounts with bulk purchase for educational, business, or sales promotional use. For information, please write to: Special Sales Department, Andrews McMeel Publishing, LLC, 1130 Walnut Street, Kansas City, Missouri 64106.

DOONESBURY.COM'S
The WAR in QUOTES

Also from Doonesbury.com

The Sandbox: Dispatches from Troops in Iraq and Afghanistan

"We're an empire now, and when we act, we create our own reality. We're history's actors, and you, all of you, will be left to just study what we do."

—Bush adviser, summer 2002

Contents

Introduction
by G. B. Trudeau

In the fall of 2007, four and a half years into the Iraq War, I was struck by how Doonesbury.com's daily *Say What?* feature had inadvertently created a remarkable collection of quotes that, when viewed in sequence, tracked the essential story of the war's unfolding.

Bush-watchers like *Slate*'s Jacob Weisberg have spent years archiving the forty-third president's innumerable "Bushisms," the strange and surprising things he did not mean to say. These can be revealing, and sometimes alarming, but *The War in Quotes* focuses on a different part of the record— words that were deliberately spoken, not only by President George W. Bush, but also by the core group who helped plan and execute the war, and by others who have been involved in various ways.

Building on our initial set of quotes, our site's Duty Officer, David Stanford, and I combed through the numerous books on the war that have been written by participants, journalists, historians, and biographers, gathering more, and roamed the Net as well. We also generated a timeline as a reminder of all that has transpired over the past seven years.

We ended up with an impressive surfeit of material. The first rough version of the book, laid out on the floor of the studio, wound from room to room and down a long hallway. By rigorous tightening the text has been reduced to its essential core.

It speaks for itself.

The Players

 George W. Bush—President of the United States

 George H. W. Bush—President of the United States, 1989–1993

 Dick Cheney—Vice president of the United States

 Donald Rumsfeld—Secretary of defense, 2001–2006

 Condoleezza Rice—National security adviser, 2001–2005; secretary of state, 2005–present

 Colin Powell—Secretary of state, 2001–2005

 Paul Wolfowitz—Deputy secretary of defense, 2001–2005

 Richard Perle—Defense Policy Board Advisory Committee, 1997–2004

Douglas Feith—Under secretary of defense for policy, 2001–2005

Paul Bremer—Second director of reconstruction and humanitarian assistance in Iraq, 2003–2004

Tony Blair—Prime minister of Great Britain, 1997–2007

Ari Fleischer—White House press secretary, 2001–2003

Dick Armey—House majority leader, 1995–2003

Gen. Richard B. Myers—Chairman, Joint Chiefs of Staff, 2001–2005

Gen. David Petraeus—Commanding general, Multi-National Force—Iraq

John McCain—U.S. senator

Humility

"I'm going to be judicious as to how I use the military.
It needs to be in our vital interest, the mission needs
to be clear, and the exit strategy obvious."
—George W. Bush, October 11, 2000

"I think one way for us to end up being viewed as the
ugly American is for us to go around the world saying,
'We do it this way. So should you.'"
—George W. Bush, October 11, 2000

"If we're an arrogant nation, they'll resent us.
If we're a humble nation but strong, they'll welcome us."
—George W. Bush, on foreign policy, October 12, 2000

September 11, 2001
2,973 killed in terrorist
attacks in U.S.

September 12, 2001
Le Monde declares "We are
all Americans"

October 7, 2001
Bush announces Operation
Enduring Freedom, aimed at
Taliban in Afghanistan

"Every nation, in every region, now has a decision to make. Either you are with us, or you are with the terrorists."
—George W. Bush, September 20, 2001

October 8, 2001
Office of Homeland
Security established

October 9, 2001
Letters carrying anthrax
mailed to U.S. senators

Foresight

"Suicide bomber(s) belonging to al-Qaeda's Martyrdom Battalion could crash-land an aircraft packed with high explosives into the Pentagon, the Central Intelligence Agency, or the White House."
—National Intelligence Council report, September 1999

"I don't think anybody could have predicted that these people would take an airplane and slam it into the World Trade Center."
—Condoleezza Rice, May 17, 2002

October 25, 2001
Senate passes Patriot Act,
98–1

November 6, 2001
First episode of *24*
airs on Fox

c. November 30, 2001
Battle of Tora Bora in Afghanistan;
Osama bin Laden escapes

"The president did not—not—receive information about the use of airplanes as missiles by suicide bombers."
—Ari Fleischer, September 11, 2001

"Bin Laden Determined to Strike in U.S."
—Presidential Daily Brief, August 2001

"An explosive title on a non-explosive piece."
—Condoleezza Rice, commenting later

"All right, you've covered your ass now."
—George W. Bush, to the CIA briefer who warned him about an imminent bin Laden strike, August 6, 2001

January 11, 2002
First detainees arrive at
Guantanamo Bay, Cuba

January 18, 2002
Bush decides terrorist status
disqualifies Gitmo detainees from
Geneva Convention protection

January 23, 2002
Wall Street Journal reporter
Daniel Pearl kidnapped in
Pakistan

7

That Was Then

"Once you've got Baghdad, it's not clear what you do with it. It's not clear what kind of government you put in place. How much credibility is that government going to have if it's set up by the U.S. military?"
—Dick Cheney, 1991

"If you get into the business of committing U.S. forces on the ground in Iraq, to occupy the place, my guess is I'd probably still have people there today."
—Dick Cheney, 1992

"How many additional dead Americans was Saddam worth? Our judgment was not very many, and I think we got that right."
—Dick Cheney, 1994

"Once you got to Iraq and took it over, and took down Saddam Hussein's government, then what are you going to put in its place? If you take down the central government of Iraq you can easily end up seeing pieces of Iraq fly off. It's a quagmire if you go that far and try to take over Iraq."
—Dick Cheney, April 15, 1994

January 29, 2002
In State of the Union address, Bush dubs Iraq, Iran, and North Korea an "axis of evil"

February 7, 2002
Justice Department memo concludes Taliban not entitled to POW status

February 21, 2002
State Department confirms killing of Daniel Pearl by Islamic militants

"I thought the decision was sound at the time, and I do today."

—Dick Cheney, on not invading Iraq, 2000

February 26, 2002
Former Ambassador Joseph Wilson
goes to Niger to explore claim Saddam
tried to obtain uranium there

February 27, 2002
Gitmo hunger strikers
protest rule against turbans;
U.S. officials relent

9

In the Name of the Father

> "I'm confident that losing men and women as a result of sniper fire inside of Baghdad would have turned the tide of public opinion very quickly."
> —George H. W. Bush, Veterans Day, 1997

> "Had we gone the invasion route, the United States could conceivably still be an occupying power in a bitterly hostile land."
> —George H. W. Bush, in his 1998 memoir

> "Trying to eliminate Saddam would have incurred incalculable human and political costs. We would have been forced to occupy Baghdad and, in effect, rule Iraq."
> —George H. W. Bush, same source

> "Whose son, whose daughter would I ask to give their lives in perhaps a fruitless hunt in Baghdad, where we could have become an occupying power? I have no regrets."
> —George H. W. Bush, 1998

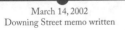

March 14, 2002
Downing Street memo written

March 28, 2002
Osama bin Laden associate
Abu Zubaydah captured in
Pakistan

April 1, 2002
State Department begins
Future of Iraq project

"You know, he is the wrong father to appeal to in terms of strength. There is a higher father that I appeal to."
—George W. Bush, asked if he'd consulted his father about Iraq, December 2003

"God told me to strike at al-Qaeda and I struck them, and then he instructed me to strike at Saddam, which I did."
—George W. Bush, as quoted by Palestinian Prime Minister Mahmoud Abbas, June 4, 2003

April 2, 2002
Capture of Zubaydah
announced

April 25, 2002
Prince Saud and Saudi
delegation dine with President
Bush in Crawford, Texas

June 1, 2002
Operation Southern Focus,
a bombing campaign against
Iraqi defenses, begins

11

Mind-set

"Dad made a mistake not going into Iraq. If I'm ever in that situation, I'll use it—I'll spend my political capital."
—George W. Bush to a family friend, 1998

"I'm just as frustrated as many Americans are that Saddam Hussein still lives."
—George W. Bush, February 16, 2000

"This is not an argument about whether to get rid of Saddam Hussein. That debate is over."
—Senior administration official, February 13, 2002

"Cheney's going to inform them that the president's decision has been made and will be carried out."
—Senior official, re: Cheney's mission to eleven Mideast countries, February 13, 2002

June 2, 2002
In West Point speech, President Bush introduces doctrine of preemptive war

August 5, 2002
Gen. Tommy Franks gives updated Iraq war plan to president

September 16, 2002
Iraq agrees to let weapons inspectors return "without conditions"; administration dismisses the offer

"Fuck Saddam. We're taking him out."
—George W. Bush, to three U.S. senators, March 2002

"I don't like motherfuckers who gas their own people. I don't like assholes who lie to the world. I'm going to kick his sorry motherfucking ass all over the Mideast."
—George W. Bush, May 1, 2002

"Bush had made up his mind to take military action."
—British Foreign Secretary Jack Straw,
re: July 23, 2002, meeting, as reported in minutes

"You'll see all this diplomatic stuff, but it's clear we're going to war."
—Senior U.S. intelligence official in Bahrain,
to colleagues, September 2002

September 20, 2002
Bush announces support for
9/11 Commission

October 10, 2002
House passes resolution
on use of force in Iraq

October 11, 2002
Senate passes resolution
on use of force in Iraq

13

"Bush didn't give a fuck about the intelligence. He had his mind made up."
—Former CIA officer, describing the president's reaction to September 17, 2002, CIA briefing on intelligence that Saddam Hussein had no weapons of mass destruction (WMDs)

"Do you want to know what the foreign policy of Iraq is to the United States? [*Gives the finger.*] Fuck the United States! That's what it is— and that's why we're going to get him."
—George W. Bush, congressional breakfast, September 2002

"Let me put it this way: If you want to see Baghdad, you'd better visit soon."
—Karl Rove, to friends, September 2002

"Penciled in for 10 March."
—George W. Bush, on invasion, to Tony Blair, January 31, 2003

October 21, 2002
Saddam Hussein
empties his prisons

November 8, 2002
U.N. passes Resolution 1441,
calling for Iraq to disarm or face
"serious consequences"

November 25, 2002
Homeland Security Act signed,
establishing Department of
Homeland Security

"I've not made up my mind about military action."
—George W. Bush, addressing the nation, March 6, 2003

"Jeez, what a fixation about Iraq."
—Colin Powell, re: George W. Bush,
during meetings shortly after 9/11

"[Saddam Hussein] has not developed any significant capability with respect to weapons of mass destruction."
—Colin Powell, February 2, 2001

"You are going to be the proud owner of twenty-five million people. You will own all their hopes, aspirations, and problems. It's going to suck the oxygen out of everything. This will become the first term."
—Colin Powell, to George W. Bush, August 14, 2002

"I'm not reading this. This is crazy."
—Colin Powell, on terrorism section of draft U.N. presentation, subsequently pared down, February 1, 2003

December 2, 2002
DOD memo approves Gitmo
interrogation techniques

January 9, 2003
Weapons inspector Hans Blix
tells U.N. no "smoking guns"
have been found

January 20, 2003
Presidential directive
assigns control over post-
war Iraq to Pentagon

Rice

"I thought he had just an incredibly inquisitive mind. You could barely finish an explanation before he was digging into it."
—Condoleezza Rice, on George W. Bush

"Do you think we should do this?"
—Bush to Rice, December 21, 2002
"Yes."
—Rice to Bush

"As I was telling my husb—as I was telling President Bush."
—Condoleezza Rice, at a dinner party, February 26, 2004

"Don't upset him."
—Condoleezza Rice, warning a foreign diplomat not to give Bush bad news, 2005

"The most powerful woman in the history of the world."
—Bush, describing Rice, May 28, 2004

January 27, 2003
IAEA head tells U.N. that inspectors have found no evidence of nuclear weapons programs in Iraq

January 28, 2003
In State of the Union address, Bush includes discredited claim that Iraq sought uranium in Africa

Where's Osama?

"The most important thing is for us to find Osama bin Laden. It is our number-one priority and we will not rest until we find him."
—George W. Bush, September 13, 2001

"Dead or alive. We're going to get him."
—George W. Bush, December 14, 2001

"I don't know where he is and I really don't care. It's not that important. It's not our priority."
—George W. Bush, May 13, 2002

"Gosh, I just don't think I ever said I'm not worried about Osama bin Laden. It's kind of one of those exaggerations."
—George W. Bush, October 13, 2004

February 5, 2003
Colin Powell addresses
U.N. seeking multination
authorization for invasion

March 1, 2003
U.S. announces "diplomacy has
failed," urges U.N. weapons
inspectors to leave Iraq

March 17, 2003
Bush gives Saddam and his
sons 48 hours to leave

"I've not heard hide nor hair of him since December."
—Donald Rumsfeld, July 22, 2002

"*Newsweek* magazine says he's in the mountains of western Pakistan. And I guess if *Newsweek* could find him there, we could, too."
—Gen. Wesley Clark, January 8, 2004

"It's a success that hasn't occurred yet."
—Homeland security adviser Fran Townsend, on the failure to capture Osama bin Laden, December 28, 2006

"I will screw him in the ass."
—George W. Bush, according to Israeli Prime Minister Ariel Sharon

March 19, 2003
Operation Iraqi Freedom begins with
air strikes in Baghdad; ground troops
invade from Kuwait

19

"We're under attack because we love freedom, is why we're under attack. And our enemy hates freedom. They hate and we love. We differ from our enemy because we love. We not only love our freedoms and love our values, we love life itself. Our enemy hates innocent life."
—George W. Bush, addressing schoolchildren, September 23, 2002

"This is a man who cannot stand what we stand for. He hates the fact, like al-Qaeda does, that we love freedom. See, they can't stand that."
—George W. Bush, on Saddam, October 31, 2002

"They hate things; we love things. They act out of hatred; we don't seek revenge, we seek justice out of love."
—George W. Bush, August 29, 2002

March 23, 2003
Pfc. Jessica Lynch
rescued in Nasiriyah

April 9, 2003
Baghdad falls; Saddam
statue pulled down

**"I hate Saddam Hussein, and I don't hate a lot of people.
I have nothing but hatred in my heart for him."**
—George H. W. Bush, fall 2002

April 10, 2003
Looting becomes rampant, especially in
Basra and in Baghdad, where government
and public buildings are plundered

April 2003
After fall of Tikrit,
Pentagon declares major
fighting in Iraq is over

21

The Al-Qaeda Connection

"No."
—Dick Cheney, asked whether there's any evidence
to tie Saddam Hussein to 9/11, September 16, 2001

"Bullet-proof."
—Ari Fleischer, on evidence of Saddam–al-Qaeda ties,
September 26, 2002

"We know he's got ties with al-Qaeda."
—George W. Bush, November 1, 2002

**"His regime has had high-level contacts
with al-Qaeda going back a decade."**
—Dick Cheney, December 2, 2002

"The support for al-Qaeda is clear-cut."
—Paul Wolfowitz, March 5, 2003

**"You know, one of the hardest parts of my job
is to connect Iraq to the war on terror."**
—George W. Bush, September 6, 2006

April 21, 2003
Provisional Coalition Authority,
headed by Jay Garner,
established in the Green Zone

May 1, 2003
Before a banner reading MISSION
ACCOMPLISHED, President Bush announces
the end of "major combat operations"

"The enemy attacked us, Jim."
—George W. Bush, on why he invaded Iraq, to Jim Lehrer in September 2004 presidential debate

Q: "What did Iraq have to do with that?"
A: "What did Iraq have to do with what?"
Q: "The attack on the World Trade Center."
A: "Nothing."
—George W. Bush, at press conference, August 24, 2006

May 6, 2003
Paul Bremer becomes top
civil administrator in Iraq,
replacing Jay Garner

May 22, 2003
U.N. lifts economic sanctions

23

"For bureaucratic reasons we settled on one issue, weapons of mass destruction, because it was the one reason everyone could agree on."
—Paul Wolfowitz, May 9, 2003

"If the president wants to go to war, our job is to find the intelligence to allow him to do so."
—Alan Foley, director, CIA Weapons Intelligence, to staff, December 2002

"It's a slam-dunk case!"
—CIA Director George Tenet, December 21, 2002

"There is already a mountain of evidence that Saddam Hussein is gathering WMDs for the purpose of using them. And adding additional information is like adding a foot to Mount Everest."
—Ari Fleischer, September 6, 2002

"There's no debate in the world as to whether they have these weapons. We all know that. A trained ape knows that."
—Donald Rumsfeld, September 13, 2002

May 23, 2003
Bremer disbands Iraqi armed forces and the staff of the Ministry of the Interior (including the police and domestic security forces)—670,000 people

May 28, 2003
Defiant letter to Iraqi people proves Saddam Hussein still alive

"Facing clear evidence of peril, we cannot wait for the final proof—the smoking gun—that could come in the form of a mushroom cloud."
—George W. Bush, October 7, 2002

"We don't want the smoking gun to be a mushroom cloud."
—Condoleezza Rice, September 8, 2002

"We know he has been absolutely devoted to trying to acquire nuclear weapons, and we believe he has, in fact, reconstituted nuclear weapons."
—Dick Cheney, March 16, 2003

"I don't believe anyone that I know in the administration ever said that Iraq had nuclear weapons."
—Donald Rumsfeld, May 14, 2003

Marketing

"From a marketing point of view, you don't roll out new products in August."
—White House Chief of Staff Andrew Card, on selling the war, September 7, 2002

"Iraq has stepped up its quest for nuclear weapons and has embarked on a worldwide hunt for materials to make an atomic bomb."
—Judith Miller and Michael Gordon, *New York Times*, September 8, 2002

"There's a story in the *New York Times* this morning. It's now public that, in fact, he has been seeking to acquire the kinds of tubes that are necessary to build a centrifuge."
—Dick Cheney, on *Meet the Press*, September 8, 2002

"We do know that there have been shipments going into Iraq of aluminum tubes that are only really suited for nuclear weapons programs."
—Condoleezza Rice, on CNN's *Late Edition*, same day

"Imagine a September 11th with weapons of mass destruction."
—Donald Rumsfeld, on *Face the Nation*, same day

July 16, 2003
Head of military ops acknowledges
U.S. seems to be facing a "classic
guerrilla-type campaign"

July 22, 2003
Saddam sons Uday and
Qusay killed in Mosul

26

"My job was not to collect information and analyze it independently; my job was to tell readers of the *New York Times* what people inside the government were saying."
—Judith Miller, February 3, 2004

"Looking back, we wish we had been more aggressive in re-examining the claims."
—*New York Times* editorial, May 27, 2004

"WMD—I got it totally wrong. If your sources are wrong, you are wrong."
—Judith Miller, October 16, 2005

"I'm deeply sorry that the stories were wrong."
—Judith Miller, November 30, 2005

August 7, 2003
Massive car bomb outside
Jordanian embassy in Baghdad
kills at least 11

August 19, 2003
Bomb destroys U.N. headquarters in Baghdad,
killing at least 20, including top U.N. envoy
Sergio Vieira de Mello

Friends

"Almost no one disagrees with these basic facts. That he has weapons of mass destruction and that he is doing everything in his power to get nuclear weapons."
—Sen. John Edwards, September 12, 2002

"In the four years since the inspectors left, intelligence reports show that Saddam Hussein has worked to rebuild his chemical and biological weapons stock, his missile delivery capability, and his nuclear program. He has also given aid, comfort, and sanctuary to terrorists, including al-Qaeda members."
—Sen. Hillary Clinton, October 10, 2002

"Saddam Hussein certainly has chemical and biological weapons. There's no question about that."
—Rep. Nancy Pelosi, November 17, 2002

August 22, 2003
U.S. announces capture of Ali Majid, "Chemical Ali"

August 29, 2003
Saddam loyalists blamed for blast killing Shia leader Ayatollah Mohammed Baqir al-Hakim

August 29, 2003
Bremer's office pledges to produce pre-war levels of electricity by October 1

"We have known for many years that Saddam Hussein is seeking and developing weapons of mass destruction."
—Sen. Edward Kennedy, September 27, 2003

"If we wait for the danger to become clear, it could be too late."
—Sen. Joseph Biden, September 4, 2002

"An operation essential to American security."
—From one of nine pro-war editorials that appeared in the *Washington Post* in February 2003

October 16, 2003
U.N. Security Council
backs revised resolution
on Iraq's future

October 23, 2003
Eighty nations meet,
pledge billions to fund
Iraq reconstruction

October 27, 2003
Attacks kill 35 at start of
Islamic holy month of
Ramadan

The Armey You Have

"I don't believe that America will justifiably make an unprovoked attack on another nation. It would not be consistent with what we have been as a nation or what we should be as a nation."

—House Majority Leader Dick Armey, August 8, 2002

"Mr. President, if you go in there, you're likely to be stuck in a quagmire that will endanger your domestic agenda for the rest of your presidency."

—Dick Armey, September 4, 2002

"I really would appreciate it if you would not talk about this point of view in public, until you've had the full briefings I've had."

—George W. Bush, to Armey, in the White House, September 4, 2002

"Trust me on this, Dick. When I get done with this briefing, you're going to be with me."

—Dick Cheney to Armey, late September 2002

"The snake is out of his hole and I believe the president's absolutely right. We've got to go kill it, disarm it, get rid of it, remove it from a threat to the nation, to the world."

—Dick Armey, announcing he would vote for resolution authorizing the use of force against Iraq, October 7, 2002

November 2, 2003
Fifteen U.S. soldiers killed when insurgents down chopper

November 12, 2003
Attack on Italian headquarters in Nasariya kills 26

November 15, 2003
IGC announces accelerated handover timetable

30

"If I'd gotten the same briefing from President Clinton or Al Gore, I probably would have said, 'Ah, bullshit.' But you don't do that with your own people."

—Dick Armey, looking back

November 27, 2003
President Bush makes surprise
Thanksgiving Day visit to U.S.
troops in Baghdad

December 14, 2003
Saddam Hussein captured near Tikrit

31

Pushback

"What the hell is going on here? You guys say you're not going to war—you're going to war!"

—Sen. Chuck Hagel, to Colin Powell, August 27, 2002

"I can't tell you how many senior officers said to me, 'What in the hell are we doing?'"

—Marine Lt. Gen. Gregory Newbold, joint staff director of operations, summer 2002

"You're going to have to occupy Iraq for years and years. The idea that democracy will suddenly blossom is something that I can't share. Are Americans ready for this?"

—German Foreign Minister Joschka Fischer, at Munich Conference on Security Policy, February 2003

"The innocent slaughter of Muslims will create, in essence, what Osama bin Laden was unable to do, a united Islamic jihad against us."

—Rep. John Larson, on Iraq invasion, August 21, 2002

December 15, 2003
Video of Saddam having DNA collected from mouth shown on Arab TV

January 17, 2004
U.S. death toll reaches 500; 346 in combat, 154 in accidents

January 23, 2004
Weapons inspector David Kay resigns

32

"These guys don't have a clue."
—Gen. Anthony Zinni, to himself, listening to Douglas Feith
and others at Senate hearings on Future of Iraq Project,
February 11, 2003

"What is happening to this country? War appears inevitable."
—Sen. Robert Byrd, March 18, 2003

**"Our preeminent security priority—underscored repeatedly
by the president—is the war on terrorism.
An attack on Iraq at this time would seriously jeopardize,
if not destroy, the global counterterrorist campaign
we have undertaken."**
—Brent Scowcroft, chairman of President's Foreign Intelligence
Advisory Board, in *Wall Street Journal* editorial,
"Don't Attack Saddam," August 15, 2002

"He's become a pain in the ass in his old age."
—George W. Bush, on Scowcroft,
after publication of *WSJ* editorial

January 28, 2004
Kay tells Senate no WMD found, says
pre-war intelligence was "almost all wrong"

February 1, 2004
Twin bombings kill 100 at Kurdish Eid celebration

The Threat

"Some in the media have chosen to use the word 'imminent.' Those were not words we used."
—White House Spokesman Scott McClellan, January 27, 2004

"This is about imminent threat."
—Scott McClellan, February 10, 2003

"You and a few other critics are the only people I've heard use the phrase 'immediate threat.' I didn't. The president didn't."
—Donald Rumsfeld, March 14, 2004

"No terrorist state poses a greater or more immediate threat to the security of our people than the regime of Saddam Hussein in Iraq."
—Donald Rumsfeld, September 19, 2002

February 10, 2004
Police station bomb kills 45 Shia in Iskandariya

March 1, 2004
IGC agrees to temporary constitution

"There's a grave threat in Iraq."
—George W. Bush, October 2, 2002

"A threat of unique urgency."
—October 2, 2002

"The threat from Iraq stands alone."
—October 7, 2002

"A serious and growing threat."
—October 16, 2002

"A real and dangerous threat."
—October 28, 2002

"I see a significant threat."
—November 1, 2002

"Saddam Hussein is a threat."
—November 3, 2002

"Unique and urgent threat."
—November 23, 2002

"Iraq is a threat, a real threat."
—January 3, 2003

"A threat to the security of free nations."
—March 16, 2003

"He was a threat. He's not a threat now."
—July 2, 2003

"We ended the threat."
—July 17, 2003

March 2, 2004
Abu Musab al-Zarqawi
blamed for holy day blasts
that kill 180 Shia

March 8, 2004
IGC signs interim
constitution

"Time is running out."
—George W. Bush, January 21, 2003

"Time is running out."
—State Department Spokesman Richard Boucher, January 23, 2003

"Time is running out."
—National Security Adviser Condoleezza Rice, January 23, 2003

"Time is running out."
—Deputy Defense Secretary Paul Wolfowitz, January 23, 2003

March 20, 2004
Army brings charges against six MPs
for Abu Ghraib abuses

"Time is running out."
—White House Press Secretary Ari Fleischer, January 24, 2003

"Time is running out."
—White House Chief of Staff Andrew Card, January 26, 2003

"Time is running out."
—White House Communications Director Dan Bartlett, January 26, 2003

"Time is running out."
—Secretary of State Colin Powell, January 27, 2003

March 22, 2004
Maj. Gen. Geoffrey D. Miller, commander at Guantanamo Bay, is reassigned as deputy commander for detainee operations in Iraq, where he will oversee Abu Ghraib and other prisons

March 31, 2004
Four U.S. contractors killed in Sunni stronghold of Fallujah

The U.N.

"We have found to date no evidence of ongoing prohibited nuclear or nuclear-related activities in Iraq."

—Mohamed ElBaradei, director of the International Atomic Agency, reporting to the U.N., February 14, 2003

"U.N. weapons inspectors are being seriously deceived. It reminds me of the way the Nazis hoodwinked Red Cross officials."

—Richard Perle, February 23, 2003

"We know that Saddam Hussein is determined to keep his weapons of mass destruction, is determined to make more."

—Secretary of State Colin Powell, to U.N. Security Council, February 5, 2003

April 4, 2004
Shia uprising in Baghdad, Basra, Najaf; Muqtada al-Sadr aide arrested, newspaper closed; 40 supporters killed

"Ladies and gentlemen, these are not assertions. These are facts."
—Colin Powell, same speech

"He presented not opinions, not conjecture, but facts."
—Donald Rumsfeld, on Powell's U.N. speech, February 8, 2003

"The people who now doubt whether or not Saddam really has WMD programs, chemical and bacteriological in particular, are really of two types. Either they work for Saddam or they're doing a human imitation of an ostrich. There really are, I think, no other possibilities."
—former CIA director James Woolsey, on *Good Morning America* the day of Powell's speech

"It's a blot. I'm the one who presented it on behalf of the United States to the world, and [it] will always be a part of my record. It was painful. It's painful now."
—Colin Powell, looking back on his U.N. speech, September 8, 2005

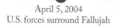

April 5, 2004
U.S. forces surround Fallujah

April 7, 2004
Laser-guided bomb targets
insurgents in Fallujah mosque

"I can't tell you if the use of force in Iraq today would last five days, or five weeks, or five months, but it certainly isn't going to last any longer than that."
—Donald Rumsfeld, November 14, 2002

"It could last six days, six weeks. I doubt six months."
—Donald Rumsfeld, February 7, 2003

"Now, it isn't going to be over in twenty-four hours, but it isn't going to be months either."
—Richard Perle, July 11, 2002

"I think it will go relatively quickly. Weeks rather than months."
—Dick Cheney, March 16, 2003

"The shooting should be over within just a very few days from when it starts."
—David Frum, February 24, 2003

"No one is talking about occupying Iraq for five to ten years."
—Richard Perle, March 9, 2003

April 15, 2004
Abu Ghraib photos leaked
to CBS, which holds story at
CIA request

April 20, 2004
Tribunal set up to try
Saddam, others

April 20, 2004
U.S. Supreme Court
hears arguments on
Guantanamo detentions

"Nobody promised a short war."
—Gen. Richard B. Myers, chairman of Joint Chiefs of Staff, March 30, 2003

"It could easily be that, absolutely."
—George W. Bush, when asked if the United States would have troops in Iraq for the next ten years, January 11, 2008

"Make it a hundred [years]. That would be fine with me."
—Sen. John McCain, on how long the United States should have troops in Iraq, January 3, 2008

"I don't think Americans are concerned if we're there for a hundred years, or a thousand years, or ten thousand years."
—John McCain, January 6, 2008

April 21, 2004
Police stations targeted in
Basra; 68 killed

April 23, 2004
Bremer eases ban on
Baathists from public sector

41

"Something on the order of several hundred thousand soldiers."
—Gen. Eric K. Shinseki, on how many troops would be needed in Iraq, testifying before the Senate Armed Services Committee, February 25, 2003

"We can say with reasonable confidence that the notion of hundreds of thousands of American troops is way off the mark."
—Paul Wolfowitz, to a Congressional committee, February 27, 2003

"I don't believe that anything like a long-term commitment of 150,000 Americans would be necessary."
—Richard Perle, October 3, 2002

"The idea that it would take several hundred thousand U.S. forces I think is far off the mark."
—Donald Rumsfeld, February 28, 2003

April 28, 2004
Images of Abu Ghraib prisoner abuse appear on *60 Minutes*

April 28, 2004
CIA Director George Tenet suspends waterboarding, other torture techniques

April 30, 2004
After a month of fighting, U.S. begins handing over Fallujah security to Iraqis; U.S. troops pull back

**"We don't have enough troops.
We don't control the terrain."**
—Colin Powell to George W. Bush and Tony Blair,
November 12, 2004

**"In my weeks in Iraq, I did not meet a single military
officer who felt, privately, that we had enough troops."**
—Coalition Provisional Authority adviser Larry Diamond,
in a memo to Condoleezza Rice, April 26, 2004

May 4, 2004
NBC News releases
executive summary of
Taguba report

May 8, 2004
Decapitated body of
American businessman
Nick Berg found

May 11, 2004
Video released showing beheading
of Berg; al-Zarqawi claims it is
revenge for prisoner abuse

43

Wolfowitz

"I think people are overly pessimistic about the aftermath."
—Paul Wolfowitz, December 2002

"I'm reasonably certain that they will greet us as liberators."
—Paul Wolfowitz, to a Congressional committee, February 27, 2003

"There's been none of the record in Iraq of ethnic militias fighting one another."
—Paul Wolfowitz, February 27, 2003

"I would expect that even countries like France will have a strong interest in assisting Iraq in reconstruction."
—Paul Wolfowitz, February 28, 2003

"To assume we're going to pay for it all is just wrong."
—Paul Wolfowitz, February 28, 2003

"We're not going to need as many people to do peacekeeping as we needed to fight the war."
—Paul Wolfowitz, April 28, 2003

May 17, 2004
Suicide bomber kills IGC
president

May 21, 2004
Spain withdraws troops
from Iraq

Feith

"Doug Feith is without question one of the most brilliant individuals in government."
—Donald Rumsfeld, August 3, 2004

"The stupidest fucking guy on the planet."
—Tommy Franks, on Feith, 2004

"Seldom in my life have I met a dumber man."
—Col. Lawrence Wilkerson, Powell's chief of staff, on Feith, October 19, 2005

"I think he's incredibly dangerous."
—Jay Garner, on Feith

"The Gestapo Office."
—Colin Powell, describing Feith's intelligence unit at the Pentagon

May 26, 2004
New York Times admits coverage of
administration claims about WMD
"not as rigorous as it should have been"

May 28, 2004
IGC names Iyad Allawi
prime minister.

Dancing in the Streets

"The Iraqi people will soon be dancing in the streets of Baghdad like those liberated in Kabul."
—Ken Adelman, Pentagon Defense Policy Board, October 6, 2002

"As I told the president on January 10th, I think [the troops] will be greeted with sweets and flowers in the first months and simply have very, very little doubt that that is the case."
—Kanan Makiya, author of *Republic of Fear*, January 10, 2003

May 30, 2004
Allawi names cabinet;
IGC dissolves itself

June 8, 2004
U.N. resolution to transfer
sovereignty to interim
Iraqi administration

"You're going to find Iraqis out cheering American troops."
—Paul Wolfowitz, February 23, 2003

"There is no question but that they would be welcomed."
—Donald Rumsfeld, February 20, 2003

"My belief is we will, in fact, be greeted as liberators."
—Dick Cheney, March 16, 2003

"Given the chance to throw off a brutal dictator like Saddam Hussein, people will rejoice."
—Ari Fleischer, March 21, 2003

June 28, 2004
Bremer transfers sovereignty
to Iraq, leaves country;
Allawi and cabinet sworn in

July 1, 2004
Saddam's first appearance
in court, charged with war
crimes and genocide

July 1, 2004
Muqtada al-Sadr takes control of
Najaf; interim government asks
coalition to remove him

47

The War Begins

"American and coalition forces are in the early stages of military operations to disarm Iraq, to free its people, and to defend the world from grave danger."
—George W. Bush, March 19, 2003

"This is the day you have been waiting for."
—U.S. military, broadcasting through Iraqi state radio after initial missile strike

July 7, 2004
Allawi signs law
allowing the declaration
of martial law

July 9, 2004
Senate report slams pre-war
intelligence, CIA, other agencies

July 15, 2004
Philippine troops begin
withdrawal to save life of
Filipino hostage

"Democracy! Whiskey! And sexy!"
—Iraqi civilian, on what liberation meant to him, April 3, 2003

July 22, 2004
9/11 Commission issues final report,
largely blaming FBI and CIA for failing
to anticipate and prevent attacks

July 28, 2004
Baquba police station
bombing kills 70

August 7, 2004
Allawi government orders
closure of Al-Jazeera
office in Baghdad

Victory

"They got it down."

—George W. Bush, watching Saddam Hussein statue
being toppled in Baghdad, April 9, 2003

"A year from now, I'll be very surprised if there is not
some grand square in Baghdad that is named after
President Bush."

—Richard Perle, September 22, 2003

"We ought to look in a mirror and get proud,
and stick out our chests, and suck in our bellies,
and say, 'Damn, we're Americans!'"

—Gen. Jay Garner, March 30, 2003

"There is, I am certain, among the Iraqi people a
respect for the care and the precision that went
into the bombing campaign."

—Donald Rumsfeld, April 9, 2003

August 18, 2004
One hundred National Assembly
members chosen by Iraqi
National Congress

August 27, 2004
Shiite militants surrender
Imam Ali mosque in Najaf

August 30, 2004
A civilian attorney visits Guantanamo
detainees, two and a half years after
the first detainees arrived

50

**"Iraqis are freer today and we are safer.
Relax and enjoy it."**
—Richard Perle, May 1, 2003

"Major combat operations are ended."
—George W. Bush, aboard USS *Abraham Lincoln,* May 1, 2003

MISSION ACCOMPLISHED.
—Banner on USS *Abraham Lincoln,* May 1, 2003

"You want to do Iran for the next one?"
—George W. Bush, on meeting with just-fired Jay Garner,
June 2, 2003

August 2004
Attacks on U.S. forces reach all-
time high, averaging 87 per day

October 7, 2004
U.S. casualties in Iraq reach 1,000;
7,000 wounded

The Army You Have

"As you know, you go to war with the army you have."
—Donald Rumsfeld, December 8, 2004

"A commander in chief leads the military built by those who came before him."
—Dick Cheney, August 30, 2000

October 7, 2004
Iraq Survey Group reports that WMD program was
destroyed in 1991, and nuke program ended, though
capability to resume retained

October 24, 2004
Forty-nine Iraqi army recruits
ambushed and executed

"Clinton's military did pretty well in Iraq, huh?"
—Comedian Al Franken, to Paul Wolfowitz at a dinner,
April 26, 2003

"Fuck you."
—Wolfowitz, in reply

November 2, 2004
President Bush elected
to second term

November 7, 2004
Offensive to retake Fallujah begins;
Allawi declares martial law

November 8, 2004
United States launches all-out
assault on Fallujah, involving
ten thousand U.S. troops

Looting

"We don't get involved in that. It's a natural process. There are some very, very angry people out there and we need to step back from that."
—Lt. Col. Eric Schwartz, commander of
U.S. Task Force 1-64, on looting and chaos, April 10, 2003

"Stuff happens."
—Donald Rumsfeld, April 11, 2003

"This is a transition period between war and what we hope will be a much more peaceful time."
—Gen. Richard B. Myers, chairman, Joint Chiefs of Staff,
April 11, 2003

"Freedom's untidy, and free people are free to make mistakes and commit crimes and do bad things. They're also free to live their lives and do wonderful things. And that's what's going to happen here."
—Donald Rumsfeld,
April 11, 2003

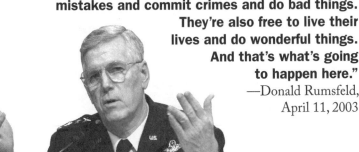

November 8, 2004
U.S. district judge declares military
commission unlawful, stops trial of
detainee Salim Ahmed Hamdan

"I picked up a newspaper and I couldn't believe it. I read eight headlines that talked about chaos, violence, unrest. And it was just Henny Penny—'The sky is falling.'"
—Donald Rumsfeld, April 11, 2003

"It is a fundamental misunderstanding to see those images over and over and over again of some boy walking out with a vase and say, 'Oh, my goodness, you don't have a plan.' That's nonsense."
—Donald Rumsfeld, April 11, 2003

"I keep reading stories about it's a country in chaos. This is simply not true. It is not a country in chaos, and Baghdad's not a city in chaos."
—Paul Bremer, August 27, 2003

November 15, 2004
After a week of fighting, U.S. and Iraqi forces retake Fallujah

November 22, 2004
Iraq general election date set for January 30, 2005

The Plan

"**Our working budgetary assumption was that ninety days after completion of the operation, we would withdraw the first fifty thousand and then every thirty days we'd take out another fifty thousand until everybody was back.**"
—Thomas E. White, former secretary of the army, on post-war planning for Iraq as ordered by Rumsfeld, mid-April 2003

"**No one had talked about what would happen when we got there. There was no plan for that. They literally told us once we got there they'd pull us back out, take us home. Once we got there it was a clusterfuck, just trying to figure out what to do.**"
—Capt. David Chasteen, 3rd Infantry Division

December 21, 2004
Suicide bomber kills 14 U.S.
soldiers at U.S. base in Mosul

December 30, 2004
Justice Department issues memo confirming that
interrogation does not have to inflict "severe physical
pain" to be torture, contradicting 2002 memo

"On the night of April 8, Col. [John] Sterling, the chief of staff of the 3rd ID, came to me and said, 'I just got off the phone with the corps chief of staff, and I asked him for the reconstruction plan, and he said there isn't one. So you've got twenty-four hours to come up with one.'"
—Col. Alan King, head of civil affairs for 3rd Infantry Division, re: April 2003

"There was no guidance for restoring order in Baghdad, creating an interim government, hiring government and essential services employees, and ensuring that the judicial system was operational."
—3rd Infantry Division's official after-action review

"[Gen. Tommy] Franks was strangely absent. He blew into Baghdad once, signed the freedom order, and left. It was like, 'I've done it, I did the offensive operations.' I really felt he was disengaged."
—Army Col. Gregory Gardner, who served at the Coalition Provisional Authority, re: May–June 2003

January 12, 2005
White House announces that
search for WMDs is over

January 14, 2005
Soldier convicted of
Abu Ghraib abuse

January 20, 2005
Abu Musab al-Zarqawi tape
posted on Islamist Web site

57

The Hunt

"We'll find them."
—Paul Wolfowitz, on the WMDs, shortly after the
fall of Baghdad, March 2003

**"As this operation continues, those weapons
will be identified, found, along with the people who have
produced them and who guard them."**
—Gen. Tommy Franks, March 22, 2003

**"I have no doubt we're going to find big
stores of weapons of mass destruction."**
—Kenneth Adelman, Defense Policy Board, March 23, 2003

**"We know where they are. They are in the area
around Tikrit and Baghdad."**
—Donald Rumsfeld, March 30, 2003

January 24, 2005
Iraq authorities reveal capture of bomber behind
blast at Baghdad U.N. headquarters

January 27, 2005
Deadliest day for U.S.
soldiers in Iraq: 36 killed

"We know that the regime has them, we know that as the regime collapses we will be led to them."
—Tony Blair, April 8, 2003

"We have high confidence that they have weapons of mass destruction. This is what this war was about and is about."
—Ari Fleischer, April 10, 2003

"We are learning more as we interrogate or have discussions with Iraqi scientists and people within the Iraqi structure, that perhaps he destroyed some, perhaps he dispersed some. And so we will find them."
—George W. Bush, April 24, 2003

"Before people crow about the absence of weapons of mass destruction, I suggest they wait a bit."
—Tony Blair, April 28, 2003

January 31, 2005
8.5 million Iraqis vote,
electing transitional government
to draft constitution

February 3, 2005
Senate confirms Alberto
Gonzales as attorney general

February 15, 2005
Gonzales signs off on secret
memo endorsing harsh
interrogation techniques

59

The Hunt (2)

"We've begun the search for hidden chemical and biological weapons and already know of hundreds of sites that will be investigated."
—George W. Bush, May 1, 2003

"We'll find them. It'll be a matter of time to do so."
—George W. Bush, May 3, 2003

"I expected them to be found.
I still expect them to be found."
—Gen. Michael Hagee, commandant of the Marine Corps, May 21, 2003

"Given time, given the number of prisoners now that we're interrogating, I'm confident that we're going to find weapons of mass destruction."
—Gen. Richard B. Myers, chairman, Joint Chiefs of Staff, May 26, 2003

February 28, 2005
Worst car bomb of war
kills 114, wounds 130,
south of Baghdad

March 3, 2005
U.S. casualties in Iraq reach 1,500

60

"They may have had time to destroy them, and I don't know the answer."
—Donald Rumsfeld, May 27, 2003

"We found the weapons of mass destruction. We found biological laboratories. For those who say we haven't found the banned manufacturing devices or banned weapons, they're wrong. We found them."
—George W. Bush, May 23, 2003

"I think that the burden is on those people who think he didn't have weapons of mass destruction to tell the world where they are."
—Ari Fleischer, July 9, 2003

April 3, 2005
Iraqi Assembly selects leaders

April 7, 2005
Kurdish leader Jalal Talabani sworn in
as interim president; Ibrahim al-Jaafari
named prime minister

61

Insurgency

"Any remaining violence is due to thugs, gangs, and terrorists."
—Donald Rumsfeld, March 14, 2004

"I really qualify it as militarily insignificant. They are very small. They are very random. They are very ineffective."
—Maj. Gen. Ray Odierno, June 18, 2003

"Pockets of dead-enders are trying to reconstitute. Gen. Franks and his team are rooting them out."
—Donald Rumsfeld, June 18, 2003

"When you take a look at the level of violence inside of Iraq, it is impossible to argue anything other than violence has, indeed, come down as a result of America's military operations."
—Ari Fleischer, June 25, 2003

"There are some who feel like that the conditions are such that they can attack us there. My answer is, bring 'em on. We've got the force necessary to deal with the security situation."
—George W. Bush, July 2, 2003

April 8, 2005
Gen. Janis Karpinski relieved of
command of 800th MP Brigade

May 1, 2005
Disclosure of 2002 Downing Street
memo; "intelligence and facts being
fixed around the policy"

"Is it a shooting gallery? Are people being shot at? Yes. Is it a difficult situation? You bet. Are more people going to be killed? I'm afraid that's true."
—Donald Rumsfeld, July 13, 2003

"We have a limited problem of some bitter-enders, some small remnants of the old regime, who are using professional military tactics to attack and kill our soldiers."
—Paul Bremer, July 20, 2003

"They pose no strategic threat to the United States or to the coalition forces."
—Paul Bremer, August 26, 2003

May 2005
Newsweek report that Gitmo interrogators flushed a Koran down a toilet touches off riots that kill 16; *Newsweek* retracts story

May 30, 2005
Cheney says insurgency in its "last throes"

Insurgency (2)

"The best way to describe the people who are conducting these attacks are cold-blooded killers, terrorists. That's all they are. They can't stand the thought of a free society. They hate freedom. They love terror."
—George W. Bush, October 27, 2003

"More people get killed in New York every night than get killed in Baghdad."
—Paul Bremer, August 2003

"Unlike other wars in the past where people talk about resistance, this resistance does not enjoy the support of the Iraqi people. Every time we get intelligence, all it takes is a platoon to go out there and clean it up. We need to project confidence. We have the people with us."
—Paul Wolfowitz, September 9, 2003

May 31, 2005
A post-election surge of violence kills 672 civilians in May, up from 364 the month before

"You know, the country is basically peaceful."
—Paul Bremer, September 24, 2003

June 14, 2005
Massoud Barzani sworn in
as regional president of Iraqi
Kurdistan

July 15, 2005
Court of Appeals overturns 2004
order and upholds Bush's authority
to create military commissions

"Detainee began to cry. Urinated on himself. Began to cry. Asked God for forgiveness. Cried. Cried. Became violent. Began to cry. Broke down and cried. Began to pray and openly cried. Cried out to Allah several times. Trembled uncontrollably."

—From a Guantanamo interrogation log, 2003

"[The show] was hugely popular. [Jack Bauer] gave people lots of ideas."

—Diane Beaver, staff judge advocate at Guantanamo, on Fox's *24*

"The inmates at Guantanamo have never been treated better and they've never been more comfortable in their lives. And the idea that somehow we are torturing people in Guantanamo is absolutely not true, unless you consider having to eat chicken three times a week is torture."

—Rep. Duncan Hunter, chairman, House Armed Services Committee, June 12, 2005

July 19, 2005
Report by U.K. group says 25,000 civilians have been killed, more than one-third by coalition forces

August 7, 2005
Cindy Sheehan begins protest in Crawford, Texas, demanding meeting with President Bush

"If I read this to you and did not tell you that it was an FBI agent describing what most Americans had done to prisoners in their control, you would most certainly believe this must have been done by Nazis, Soviets in their gulags, or some mad regime—Pol Pot or others— that had no concern for human beings."
—Sen. Dick Durbin, re: FBI agent report on treatment of Gitmo prisoners, June 17, 2005

"Someone is chained to a floor and forced to defecate on themselves, and has loud rock music playing. Excuse me? I mean, you know, Auschwitz? Bergen-Belsen? The Soviet gulag? I think they would have been very happy to be allowed to defecate on themselves."
—Fox News' Chris Wallace, re: Durbin's Gitmo comments, June 17, 2005

"Wait a minute, we can't have acquittals. If we've been holding these guys for so long, how can we explain letting them get off? We can't have acquittals. We've got to have convictions."
—Pentagon general counsel William Haynes to Col. Morris Davis, Gitmo chief prosecutor, August 2005

August 28, 2005
Draft constitution approved
by Kurd and Shia negotiators,
rejected by Sunnis

August 31, 2005
Almost 1,000 killed in
stampede of Shia pilgrims

September 14–September 16, 2005
Hundreds killed in three days of
bombings and shootings

"If the word of how they're being treated keeps getting out, we're going to have al-Qaeda people surrendering all over the world trying to get in the place."
—Radio commentator Rush Limbaugh, June 16, 2005

"It would make a beautiful resort."
—Sen. Jeff Sessions, June 15, 2005

"I know of no one in the U.S. government, in the executive branch, that is considering closing Guantanamo."
—Donald Rumsfeld, June 8, 2005

September 19, 2005
British troops storm police station to free U.K. soldiers being held by Iraqi police

September 28, 2005
U.S. soldier sentenced to three years for Abu Ghraib abuses

September 29, 2005
Bomb attacks in Balad kill 62

"We're looking at all alternatives and have been."
—George W. Bush, asked if Guantanamo should be shut down, June 8, 2005

October 5, 2005
U.K. accuses Iran of aiding Shia
insurgents in Iraq

October 12, 2005
Gen. Karpinski publishes memoir blaming
contractors and superiors, including
Rumsfeld, for Abu Ghraib abuse

69

Saddam Captured

"A piece of trash waiting to be collected."
—Colin Powell, on Saddam Hussein, July 30, 2003

"Ladies and gentlemen, we got him."
—Paul Bremer, announcing the capture of Saddam Hussein,
December 14, 2003

**"Here was a man who was photographed hundreds
of times shooting off rifles and showing how tough he
was, and in fact, he wasn't very tough, he was cowering in
a hole in the ground, and had a pistol and didn't use it
and certainly did not put up any fight at all.
In the last analysis, he seemed not terribly brave."**
—Donald Rumsfeld, December 14, 2003

**"My name is Saddam Hussein. I am the president of Iraq,
and I want to negotiate."**
—Saddam, to U.S. troops who captured him, December 14, 2003

October 15, 2005
Millions vote, approving Iraq's new
constitution despite Sunni opposition,
making Iraq an Islamic federal democracy

October 16, 2005
U.S. air strikes kill
70 near Ramadi

"I wish things were like when Ronald Reagan was still president."
—Saddam Hussein, according to one of his guards

October 19, 2005
Saddam trial begins; he is accused of war crimes and crimes against humanity in the killing of 143 Shia men in 1982

October 25, 2005
U.S. casualties in Iraq reach 2,000

The Hunt Ends

"U.S. officials never expected that we were going to open garages and find weapons of mass destruction."
—Condoleezza Rice, May 12, 2003

"I'm not concerned about weapons of mass destruction. I didn't come [to Iraq] on a search for weapons of mass destruction."
—Paul Wolfowitz, July 22, 2003

"I cannot stress too much that the president was the one in the room who was the least unhappy and the least disappointed about the lack of WMDs."
—David Kay, chief WMD hunter, July 28, 2003

"What went wrong? Why did we get it so wrong?"
—George W. Bush, to David Kay after Kay reported to the Senate that WMD claims had been "all wrong," January 2004

October 30, 2005
Pentagon estimates at least 26,000
Iraqis killed/injured January
2004–September 2005

November 2, 2005
Washington Post reports on covert prison system
set up by CIA after 9/11, used for interrogating
al-Qaeda suspects in Eastern Europe

"We are still looking. We are still searching."
—Colin Powell, January 14, 2004

**"Those weapons of mass destruction
have got to be somewhere!"**
—George W. Bush, joking about the failure to find WMDs in Iraq,
while narrating a comic slide show for the Radio and Television
Correspondents' Association dinner, March 25, 2004

November 2005
CIA destroys tapes of interrogation
of Abu Zubaydah and Abd
al-Rahim al-Nashiri

November 10, 2005
Senate approves amendment
to deny detainees right to file
habeas corpus petitions

73

"Democracy is on the march in this country.
And it's on the march at the grassroots level,
where it really matters."
—Paul Bremer, September 5, 2003

"We've got this under control."
—Gen. John Abizaid, September 9, 2003

"While there is no question we have faced some
challenges and we've got some ahead of us, we have
really achieved numerous successes and expect
the situation to continue to improve."
—Gen. Richard B. Myers, in a Pentagon news conference,
October 2, 2003

November 17, 2005
Rep. John Murtha calls for immediate
withdrawal of U.S. troops from Iraq

"Listen, we're making good progress in Iraq.
Sometimes it's hard to tell it when you listen to the filter.
We're making good progress."
—George W. Bush, October 6, 2003

"Things are going better than they could have
been expected to go at this time, and we're
making great progress."
—Andrew Card, December 7, 2003

"We think the insurgency is waning. The ones who
continue to fight are losing their support."
—Brig. Gen. Mark Hertling, November 7, 2003

November 22, 2005
Memo reveals Bush told Tony Blair in April 2004
he was considering bombing Al-Jazeera; Blair said
to have talked him out of it

Abu Ghraib

"We are treating the Iraqi prisoners extremely well. In fact, I think they get good food and shelter and they're free from the horrible commanders they used to work for. I think most of them are much happier, frankly."
—Paul Wolfowitz, March 23, 2003

"For many, living conditions are now better in prison than at home. At one point we were concerned they wouldn't want to leave."
—Brig. Gen. Janis Karpinski, December 14, 2003

"Numerous incidents of sadistic, blatant, and wanton criminal abuses."
—From report on Abu Ghraib by Gen. Antonio Taguba, May 2004

"Some assholes have just lost the war for us."
—Nineteen-year-old lance corporal in Iraq, to Maj. Gen. James Mattis, upon seeing Abu Ghraib story on TV, April 2004

"The Christian in me says it's wrong, but the corrections officer in me says, 'I love to make a grown man piss himself.'"
—Spc. Charles Graner, Abu Ghraib guard, May 22, 2004

December 15, 2005
Eleven million turn out for election of full-term parliament: 7,000 candidates from 300 parties compete for 275 seats

December 16, 2005
New York Times story reveals secret NSA domestic eavesdropping program

December 30, 2005
Bush signs McCain torture ban, along with statement that negates it

"Why would I want to go see a bunch of perverted pictures?"
—Sen. Trent Lott, declining viewing opportunity for senators to look at the 1,800 Abu Ghraib photographs, May 12, 2004

"Don't cheerleaders all over America form pyramids six to eight times a year? Is that torture?"
—Defense attorney at Abu Ghraib trial, January 10, 2005

"I'm talking about people having a good time, these people, you ever heard of emotional release? You ever heard of need to blow some steam off?"
—Rush Limbaugh, on Abu Ghraib, May 4, 2004

January 21, 2006
Shia-led United Iraqi Alliance announced as winner of December election

February 22, 2006
Bomb damages Golden Dome mosque, sparking reprisals against Sunnis

March 13, 2006
U.K. announces it will reduce troop strength from 7,800 to 7,000

77

"I think we're on the brink of success."
—Gen. Richard B. Myers, to House Armed Services Committee,
May 21, 2004

"Frankly, part of our problem is a lot of the press
are afraid to travel very much, so they sit in Baghdad
and they publish rumors. And rumors are plentiful."
—Paul Wolfowitz, to House Armed Services Committee,
June 24, 2004

"I think they're in the last throes, if you will,
of the insurgency."
—Dick Cheney, July 20, 2005

March 19, 2006
Time reveals that in Haditha in
November 2005, U.S. marines killed
24 Iraqis, including 17 civilians

"What is he, some kind of defeatist?"
—George W. Bush, on Baghdad CIA station chief whose report detailed how U.S. mishaps had destabilized the country and fueled the insurgency, and predicted more than two thousand U.S. casualties, December 2004

"My fellow citizens: Not only can we win the war in Iraq, we *are* winning the war in Iraq."
—George W. Bush, August 17, 2005

"We're on the road to victory here."
—George W. Bush, November 19, 2005

"See, in my line of work you have to keep repeating things over and over and over again for the truth to sink in, to kind of catapult the propaganda."
—George W. Bush,
May 24, 2005

Civil War

"There's been a certain amount of pop sociology in America, that the Shia can't get along with the Sunni and the Shia in Iraq just want to establish some kind of Islamic fundamentalist regime. There's almost no evidence of that at all. Iraq's always been very secular."
—Commentator William Kristol, April 1, 2003

"The terrorists in Iraq failed to incite an Iraqi civil war."
—George W. Bush, June 28, 2005

"When I think civil war, I think Antietam, Gettysburg. I don't think we're there yet."
—Dick Cheney, October 25, 2006

April 19, 2006
DOD releases names of 558
Guantanamo detainees

"For months now the White House has rejected claims that the situation in Iraq has deteriorated into civil war. After careful consideration, NBC News has decided that the situation in Iraq, with armed militarized factions fighting for their own political agendas, can now be characterized as civil war."
—Matt Lauer on *Today,* November 27, 2006

"ALL-OUT CIVIL WAR IN IRAQ: COULD IT BE A GOOD THING?"
—Fox News headline, February 23, 2006

"Why do they hate each other? Why do Sunnis kill Shiites? How do they tell the difference? They all look the same to me."
—Sen. Trent Lott, September 28, 2006

"It's hard for me, living in this beautiful White House, to give you a firsthand assessment. I haven't been there. You have. I haven't."
—George W. Bush, asked by ABC reporter Martha Raddatz if there is a civil war in Iraq, February 14, 2007

April 21, 2006
After months of deadlock,
Nouri al-Maliki appointed
prime minister

May 6, 2006
Five U.K. personnel killed
in Basra chopper crash

May 20, 2006
Al-Maliki oversees formation
of first post-Saddam permanent
constitutional government

81

Fallujah I

> **"I want heads to roll."**
> —George W. Bush, on learning of the killing of four contractors,
> March 31, 2004

> **"I don't care about the people of Fallujah. You're not going to win their hearts and minds. Let's knock the place down."**
> —Fox News commentator Bill O'Reilly, March 31, 2004

> **"Kick ass! If somebody tries to stop the march to democracy, we will seek them out and kill them! Our will is being tested, but we are resolute. We have a better way. Stay strong! Stay the course! Kill them! Be confident! Prevail! We are going to wipe them out! We are not blinking!"**
> —George W. Bush, during a White House videoconference
> re: the first battle for Fallujah, April 6, 2004

> **60%–70%**
> —Percentage of Fallujah's buildings estimated
> to have been destroyed in fighting
> **20%**
> —Percentage suffering major damage

> **"Most of Fallujah is returning to normal."**
> —George W. Bush, April 28, 2004

June 7, 2006
U.S. air strike kills al-Zarqawi,
leader of al-Qaeda in Iraq and
figurehead of Sunni insurgency

June 10, 2006
Three Guantanamo
detainees commit suicide

June 15, 2006
U.S. casualties in Iraq
reach 2,500

Fallujah II

"All fighters in Fallujah should surrender, and we guarantee they will not be killed or insulted."
—American psychological operations message broadcast from Humvee-mounted loudspeakers, November 2004

"We ask the American soldiers to surrender, and we guarantee that we will kill and torture them."
—Insurgent response over mosque loudspeaker

June 20, 2006
Mutilated bodies of two
U.S. soldiers found in
Youssifiyah

June 29, 2006
Supreme Court rules that commissions
violate U.S. and international law, and that
Geneva Conventions apply to detainees

July 1, 2006
Car bomb kills 66
in Sadr City

83

Torture

"The war against terrorism is a new kind of war. In my judgment, this new paradigm renders obsolete Geneva's strict limitations on questioning of enemy prisoners and renders quaint some of its provisions."
—White House counsel Alberto Gonzales, in a memo to George W. Bush, January 2002

"To be considered torture, techniques must produce lasting psychological damage or suffering 'equivalent in intensity to the pain accompanying serious physical injury, such as organ failure, impairment of bodily function, or even death.'"
—Deputy Assistant Attorney General John Yoo and Justice Department counsel Robert Delahunty, in memo, January 9, 2002

"I note that, because Geneva does not apply to our conflict with al-Qaeda, al-Qaeda detainees also do not qualify as prisoners of war."
—George W. Bush, memo, February 7, 2002

July 13, 2006
U.K. hands over security in Muthanna province to local forces

July 18, 2006
Car bomb kills 53 near Shia shrine in Kufa

July 27, 2006
Saddam's first trial ends after nine months

"I stand 8–10 hours a day. Why is standing limited to 4 hours?"
—Donald Rumsfeld, in comment scrawled on an interrogation technique memo, 2002

"Why are we talking about this in the White House? History will not judge this kindly."
—Attorney General John Ashcroft, on torture being micromanaged in the White House basement by Dick Cheney, Condoleezza Rice, Colin Powell, George Tenet, Donald Rumsfeld, and himself

"I'm aware our National Security team met on this issue. And I approved."
—George W. Bush, June 2008

August 3, 2006
CENTCOM commander
Gen. John Abizaid says Iraq
civil war is possible

August 16, 2006
NYT reports that 1,666 bombs
exploded in Iraq in July,
highest monthly total to date

85

Torture (2)

"Look, I'm gonna say it one more time. I can—if I can—maybe—maybe I can be more clear. The instructions went out to our people to adhere to law. That oughta comfort you. We—we're a nation of law. We adhere to laws. We have laws on the books. You might look at those laws. And that might provide comfort for you. And those were the instructions out of—from me to the government."
—George W. Bush, asked if torture is ever justified, June 10, 2004

"The problem with moral authority is people who should know better siding with the assholes."
—Douglas Feith, asked if he was concerned that torture might have diminished America's moral authority, May 2008

"Congress doesn't have the power to tie the president's hands in regard to torture as an interrogation technique. It's the core of the commander-in-chief function. They can't prevent the president from ordering torture."
—John Yoo, former deputy assistant attorney general, 2005

"No president has done more for human rights than I have."
—George W. Bush, January 20, 2004

"What does this mean? 'Outrages upon human dignity?'"
—George W. Bush, September 15, 2006

August 31, 2006
Saddam trial begins for campaign that killed 180,000 Kurds in the 1980s

September 7, 2006
U.S. announces partial handover of Iraqi navy and air force

September 20, 2006
U.N. report estimates more Iraqis died in July–August than in May–June

86

Waterboarding

"A no-brainer."
—Dick Cheney, on waterboarding, October 24, 2006

"Well, I'm not sure it is either. I'm not sure it is either. It depends on how it's done. It depends on the circumstances. It depends on who does it."
—Rudy Giuliani, on waterboarding not being torture, October 24, 2007

"There are different ways of doing it. It's like swimming—freestyle, backstroke."
—Sen. Kit Bond, asked if waterboarding is torture, December 11, 2007

"It is not like putting burning coals on people's bodies. The person is in no real danger. The impact is psychological."
—Sen. Joe Lieberman, after voting against a bill prohibiting waterboarding, February 14, 2008

"We got more information out of a German general with a game of chess or Ping-Pong than they do today, with their torture."
—Henry Kolm, 90, part of a U.S. intelligence team that interrogated Nazi POWs during WWII

September 21, 2006
Italian troops withdraw from
Iraq, handing control of Dhi Qar
province to Iraqi troops

September 26, 2006
Release of partially
declassified April 2006 NIE
"Trends in Global Terrorism"

87

The Mission

"Our mission is clear in Iraq. Should we have to go in, our mission is very clear: disarmament."
—George W. Bush, March 6, 2003

"Our mission is clear: to train the Iraqis so they can do the fighting and make sure they can stand up to defend their freedoms, which they want to do."
—George W. Bush, June 2, 2005

"Our mission in Iraq is clear. We're hunting down the terrorists. We're helping Iraqis build a free nation that is an ally in the war on terror. We're advancing freedom in the broader Middle East. We are removing a source of violence and instability, and laying the foundation of peace for our children and our grandchildren."
—George W. Bush, June 29, 2005

November 5, 2006
Saddam Hussein sentenced
to death by hanging

November 7, 2006
Democrats win control of Senate and
House in midterm elections

"We have a new strategy with a new mission: helping secure the population, especially in Baghdad. Our plan puts Iraqis in the lead."
—George W. Bush, January 13, 2007

"It's a new mission. And David Petraeus is in Iraq carrying it out. Its goal is to help the Iraqis make progress toward reconciliation—to build a free nation that respects the rights of its people, upholds the rule of law, and is an ally against the extremists in this war."
—George W. Bush, June 28, 2007

November 8, 2006
Rumsfeld resigns as secretary of defense
one day after midterm elections; Bush
nominates Robert Gates to replace him

November 27, 2006
NBC News announces it
is now referring to the Iraq
conflict as a civil war

Stepping Up

"We don't need them."
—Paul Bremer, on disbanding the Iraqi army, May 2003

"The best way for Iraq to be safe and secure is for Iraqi citizens to be trained to do the job. And that's what we're doing. We've got 100,000 trained now, 125,000 by the end of this year, 200,000 by the end of next year."
—George W. Bush, September 30, 2004

"Today they have more than 100 battalions operating throughout the country."
—George W. Bush, October 1, 2005

"Right now there are over 30 Iraqi battalions in the lead."
—George W. Bush, October 4, 2005

December 6, 2006
Bipartisan Baker Commission releases Iraq Study Group report, calls situation "grave and deteriorating," urges talks with Iran and Syria

December 30, 2006
Saddam Hussein executed

January 3, 2007
U.S. casualties in Iraq reach 3,000

"Today there are more than 80 Iraqi army battalions fighting the insurgency alongside our forces."
—George W. Bush, October 6, 2005

"As Iraqis stand up, we will stand down."
—George W. Bush, December 16, 2005

"Iraqis can take over security in the next twelve to eighteen months."
—Gen. George Casey, August 29, 2006

"I can tell you that by next June, our forces will be ready."
—Iraqi Prime Minister Nouri al-Maliki, November 30, 2006

January 10, 2007
Ignoring Iraq Study Group report,
President Bush announces surge,
calling for 20,000 additional troops

January 22, 2007
More than 130 killed in
and around Baghdad

February 10, 2007
Gen. David Petraeus
takes charge as top U.S.
commander in Iraq

"I didn't advocate invasion. I wasn't asked."
—Donald Rumsfeld, November 20, 2005

"We need a better presentation to respond to this business that 'The Department of Defense had no plan.' That is just utter nonsense. We need to knock it down hard."
—Donald Rumsfeld, in a memo to Pentagon official Dorrance Smith, March 10, 2006

**"14. Keep elevating the threat.
15. Talk about Somalia, the Philippines, etc. Make sure the American people realize they are surrounded in the world by violent extremists."**
—Donald Rumsfeld, from a fifteen-point memo titled "Thoughts from My Meeting with the Military Analysts," April 19, 2006

February 21, 2007
Tony Blair announces
withdrawal of 1,600 of
U.K.'s 7,100 troops

March 8, 2007
Defense Secretary Gates
approves 2,200 more
military police for Baghdad

"Now, what is the message there? The message is that there are known 'knowns.' There are things we know that we know. There are known unknowns. That is to say there are things that we now know we don't know. But there are also unknown unknowns. There are things we don't know we don't know. So when we do the best we can and we pull all this information together, and we then say, well, that's basically what we see as the situation, that is really only the known knowns and the known unknowns. And each year, we discover a few more of those unknown unknowns."
—Donald Rumsfeld, June 6, 2002

"We have been very careful about saying what we knew and what we didn't know."
—Donald Rumsfeld, July 13, 2003

"He leads in a way that the good Lord tells him is best for our country."
—Gen. Peter Pace, defending the defense secretary, who picked him to serve as chairman of the Joint Chiefs of Staff, October 19, 2006

"He's done a heck of a job."
—George W. Bush, on Rumsfeld, December 14, 2005

March 19, 2007
Conference of Iraq's
neighbors seeks support for
its new government

March 27, 2007
Tal Afar truck
bomb kills 152

March 28, 2007
Ryan Crocker replaces
Zalmay Khalilzad as U.S.
ambassador to Iraq

93

"We are fighting these terrorists with our military in Afghanistan and Iraq and beyond so we do not have to face them in the streets of our own cities."
—George W. Bush, October 25, 2004

"I think it's a lot better for this country to be fighting terrorists in Baghdad rather than in Boston or in Baltimore or Boise."
—Donald Rumsfeld, September 14, 2003

"America is better off fighting terrorists in the streets of Baghdad than we would be fighting them in the streets of Detroit or New Orleans or San Francisco."
—Sen. Bob Bennett, September 29, 2003

"I would far rather have our troops fight these terrorists on the streets of Baghdad than our firefighters fight them on the streets of Brooklyn."
—New York Governor George Pataki, November 3, 2003

April 12, 2007
Suicide bomber kills eight inside
Iraqi parliament building

April 16, 2007
Muqtada al-Sadr orders Shia cabinet
members to resign, to pressure Maliki to
set timetable for withdrawal of U.S. troops

"We have to fight the terrorists in Baghdad so we don't have to fight them on the streets of Nashville, Tennessee."
—Maj. Gen. Rick Lynch, 3rd Infantry Division

"If we leave, they will follow us."
—Gen. John Abizaid, commander, Central Command, summer 2006

April 18, 2007
Baghdad bombings
kill almost 200

May 1, 2007
Bush vetoes war spending bill
spelling out benchmarks toward
withdrawal

June 7, 2007
U.S. casualties reach
3,500

The Surge

"Sending more Americans would undermine our strategy of encouraging Iraqis to take the lead in this fight. And sending more Americans would suggest that we intend to stay forever, when we are, in fact, working for the day when Iraq can defend itself and we can leave."
—George W. Bush, June 2006

"I've committed more than twenty thousand additional American troops to Iraq. The vast majority of them— five brigades—will be deployed to Baghdad. These troops will work alongside Iraqi units and be embedded in their formations."
—George W. Bush, announcing the troop surge, January 10, 2007

"The definition of success, as I described, is, you know, 'sectarian violence down.' Success is not 'no violence.' There are parts of our own country that have got a certain level of violence to it."
—George W. Bush, May 2, 2007

"A potential death sentence. Any other embassy in the world would be closed by now."
—A forty-six-year Foreign Service veteran, on the State Department decision to order officers to take assignments in Baghdad or risk being fired, October 31, 2007

June 7, 2007
Human rights groups' report identifies 39 "ghost prisoners" believed to be in U.S. custody

June 24, 2007
Ali Hassan al-Majid, "Chemical Ali," convicted and sentenced to death

July 2007
Bush signs new executive order authorizing "enhanced" interrogation techniques

"Things are better and there are encouraging signs. Never have I been able to go out into the city as I was today."
—Sen. John McCain, at a Baghdad press conference following a visit to a local market, April 1, 2007

"Like a normal outdoor market in Indiana in the summertime."
—Rep. Mike Pence, describing the same visit

"McCain's delegation was guarded by over 100 U.S. troops with three Blackhawk helicopters and two Apache gunships overhead. Less than 30 minutes after McCain wrapped up, a barrage of half a dozen mortars peppered the boundaries of the Green Zone, where the senators held their press conference."
—*Time*

August 1, 2007
Six Sunni members leave
cabinet, critical of Shia-led
administration

August 6, 2007
Five Sunni members
of parliament loyal to
Allawi leave cabinet

Turning Points

"We've reached another great turning point."
—George W. Bush, November 6, 2003

"A turning point will come two weeks from today."
—George W. Bush, June 16, 2004

**"The year 2005 will be recorded as a turning point
in the history of Iraq, the history of the Middle East,
and the history of freedom."**
—George W. Bush, December 12, 2005

"We believe this is a turning point for the Iraqi citizens."
—George W. Bush, May 1, 2006

**"We have now reached a turning point
in the struggle between freedom and terror."**
—George W. Bush, May 22, 2006

August 14, 2007
Over 500 Yazidis killed in attack
on the northern Iraq religious
minority group

August 16, 2007
Maliki forms Shia-Kurdish
coalition government, without
Sunni representation

August 27, 2007
Attorney General
Gonzales resigns amid
U.S. attorney scandal

"We haven't turned any corners. We haven't seen any light at the end of the tunnel."
—Gen. David Petraeus, April 8, 2008

August 29, 2007
Muqtada al-Sadr's Mahdi army
declares six-month cease-fire

September 3, 2007
Bush, Rice, and Gates make
surprise visit to Anbar province
in Iraq; Bush meets with Maliki

"It is unimaginable that the United States would have to contribute hundreds of billions of dollars and highly unlikely that we would have to contribute even tens of billions of dollars."
—Kenneth M. Pollack, National Security Council director for Persian Gulf affairs, September 2002

"The costs of any intervention would be very small."
—Glenn Hubbard, White House economic adviser, October 4, 2002

"There is a lot of money to pay for this that doesn't have to be U.S. taxpayer money. We are talking about a country that can really finance its own reconstruction and relatively soon."
—Paul Wolfowitz, March 27, 2003

September 10, 2007
Gen. Petraeus and
Ambassador Crocker testify
on Iraq before Congress

September 13, 2007
Bush announces plan to withdraw
surge troops, acknowledges U.S.
forces may be in Iraq for years

"$50 billion–$60 billion"

—Pre-invasion White House estimate of Iraq war cost

"$1.7 trillion"

—Cost estimate, by economists and Congressional Budget Office favored by White House, spring 2008

"$3 trillion"

—Projected final cost of war, according to Nobel-winning economist Joseph Stiglitz, spring 2008

"So?"

—Dick Cheney, when informed by a reporter that two-thirds of Americans do not think the Iraq war was worth the cost, March 19, 2008

September 16, 2007
Blackwater employees
kill 17 Iraqi civilians

October 8, 2007
British Prime Minister Gordon Brown
announces half the U.K.'s 5,000 troops in
Basra will be withdrawn by end of 2008

101

Me, Too

"My belief is we will in fact be greeted as liberators."
—Dick Cheney, 2003

"We will be welcomed as liberators."
—John McCain, 2003

"I think it will go relatively quickly."
—Dick Cheney, 2003

"This conflict is going to be relatively short."
—John McCain, 2003

"We will stay the course."
—George W. Bush, 2004

"We've got to stay the course."
—John McCain, 2004

October 17, 2007
Turkey authorizes cross-border
raids against Kurdish militants

December 16, 2007
Basra, last remaining province
under U.K. control, handed
over to Iraqis

"Al-Qaeda's on the run."
—George W. Bush, 2008

"Al-Qaeda's on the run."
—John McCain, 2008

"A major success."
—Dick Cheney, 2008

"The surge has succeeded."
—John McCain, 2008

December 16, 2007
Turkey launches air raids on
Kurdish fighters in northern Iraq

December 29, 2007
Gen. David Petraeus reports
car bomb and suicide attacks
down 60% since June

The Tone in Washington

"They're more interested in special interests
than they are in protecting the American people."
—George W. Bush, on Senate Democrats, November 4, 2002

"There's a group in the opposition party who are
willing to retreat. They're willing to wave the
white flag of surrender."
—George W. Bush, June 28, 2006

"The Democrat approach in Iraq comes down to this:
the terrorists win and America loses."
—George W. Bush, October 30, 2006

"The Democrats are the party of cut and run."
—George W. Bush, November 3, 2006

"It's a sad commentary on the Democrat Party that
its leaders have resorted to knee-jerk opposition."
—George W. Bush, November 5, 2006

"No matter what shortcomings these critics diagnose,
their prescription is always the same: retreat."
—George W. Bush, March 27, 2008

January 12, 2008
Iraq allows former Baath
members back into public life

February 1, 2008
Female suicide bombers in
Baghdad pet market kill 73

February 17, 2008
Turkish troops move
against Kurdish militants in
northern Iraq

"The most disappointing thing about Washington has been the name-calling. I've tried to be respectful to all parties."
—George W. Bush, December 5, 2007

February 22, 2008
Muqtada al-Sadr orders six-
month extension of cease-fire

February 29, 2008
"Chemical Ali" executed

"The army is about broken."
—Colin Powell, December 17, 2006

"72% of American troops serving in Iraq think the U.S. should exit the country within the next year."
—Le Moyne College/Zogby International poll, February 28, 2006

"The kind of debate that we've had in the United States, suggestions, for example, that we should withdraw U.S. forces from Iraq, simply validates the strategy of the terrorists."
—Dick Cheney, September 10, 2006

"This business about graceful exit just simply has no realism to it at all."
—George W. Bush, November 30, 2006

March 2, 2008
Iranian president
Mahmoud Ahmadinejad
visits Baghdad

March 7, 2008
Bomb kills 57 in Baghdad

March 13, 2008
Kidnapped Chaldean
Catholic archbishop of
Mosul found dead

"There is no substitute for victory, and withdrawal is defeat."
—John McCain, April 8, 2008

March 17, 2008
Suicide bomber kills
42 in Karbala

March 23, 2008
U.S. casualties reach 4,000

"Does [the Iraq war strategy] make America safer?"

—Sen. John Warner

March 26, 2008
Heavy fighting as Iraqi ground
forces launch operation against
militias in Basra, Baghdad

March 27, 2008
Hundreds of thousands
march in Baghdad to protest
crackdown on al-Sadr followers

March 29, 2008
U.S. conducts air strikes
in support of Iraqi forces
battling militias

"I don't know, actually."
—Gen. David Petraeus, in Senate testimony, September 11, 2007

March 31, 2008
Al-Sadr suspends
battle in Basra

April 8, 2008
Gen. Petraeus begins several
days of congressional
testimony

April 23, 2008
Petraeus named to head
Central Command

Editor's Note

To make the material read smoothly, in some instances we have taken the liberty of dispensing with ellipses when leaving out extraneous portions of quotes, taking care not to alter the speaker's meaning or strip the quote of relevant context.

A complete list of sources is posted on Doonesbury.com at www.doonesbury.com/warinquotes/sources.

Photo Credits

WITHDRAWN